D0535900

Talking About

Your Weight

By Hazel Edwards
and Goldie Alexander

Gareth Stevens
Publishing

Please visit our Web site www.garethstevens.com. For a free color catalog of all our high-quality books, call toll free 1-800-542-2595 or fax 1-877-542-2596.

Library of Congress Cataloging-in-Publication Data

Edwards, Hazel.

 Talking about your weight / Hazel Edwards and Goldie Alexander.

    p. cm. — (Healthy living)

 Includes index.

 ISBN 978-1-4339-3655-5 (lib. bdg.)

 1. Self-care, Health—Juvenile literature. 2. Body weight—Juvenile literature. 3. Weight gain—Juvenile literature. I. Alexander, Goldie, 1936- II. Title.

 RA777.E355 2010

 613—dc22

                2009043442

Published in 2010 by

Gareth Stevens Publishing

111 East 14th Street, Suite 349

New York, NY 10003

© 2010 Blake Publishing

For Gareth Stevens Publishing:

Art Direction: Haley Harasymiw

Editorial Direction: Kerri O'Donnell

Cover photo: iStockphoto

Photos and illustrations:

Australian Guide to Healthy Eating copyright Commonwealth of Australia, page 12 (food plate); iStockphoto, pages 4–30; Photos.com, pages 4–5; UC Publishing, pages 11 (bottom), 16, 20–21

Printed in the United States of America

CPSIA compliance information: Batch #CW10GS: For further information contact Gareth Stevens, New York, New York, at 1-800-542-2595.

Contents

All shapes and sizes

Variety's the very spice of life,

That gives it all its flavor.

(From *The Task* by William Cowper, English poet, 1731–1800)

People come in all shapes and sizes. That's one of life's great joys. As much as we like the secure feeling of belonging to a group, it's equally wonderful to know that we are unique. Some people are large; some people are not. So what's the big deal about weight?

The big deal

How much people weigh makes no difference in how kind they are, how clever they are, or what great friends they are. But sometimes being **overweight** or underweight can make a difference in health and wellness. Weight is not the problem; being unwell is the problem.

Making the most of our lives includes taking care of our bodies. Keeping a healthy weight and an active lifestyle helps us be the best we can. And being the best we can helps us have a happy life. That's the big deal!

Nothing new

Hundreds of years ago, humans had to hunt, gather, or grow all their food. That took a lot more **energy** than it takes to drive to the supermarket or call for a pizza delivery!

Our bodies are designed to make body fat as a way of storing energy. When food is hard to find, the stores of body fat help keep people alive. When there is plenty of food around, the need to store energy is reduced, but the body doesn't know that. Some body fat is needed to act as a cushion around our **internal organs** and guard them from harm. Sometimes, however, there is too much padding.

Concern about healthy eating is nothing new. Our language is filled with sayings about the need to respect our bodies.

One should eat to live, not live to eat.

Good health is true wealth.

Your stomach shouldn't be a "waist basket."

If an apple a day keeps the doctor away, imagine what two servings of fruit and five of vegetables a day will do!

What does "overweight" mean?

Asking how much a person should weigh is a bit like asking how long a piece of string should be. It depends! It depends on your age, your height, your gender, and your background. Remember, too, that when you weigh yourself, you're not just weighing the fat. Your weight is made up of all the parts of your body—bones, **muscles**, teeth, toenails, and all other body parts.

As children grow, their height and weight can be checked against the average height and weight of other children the same age and gender. If they weigh a lot more than the average, they may be overweight.

Being overweight is bad news for both your mind and your body!

Overweight people are more likely to:
- feel tired
- have breathing problems
- have sleeping problems
- strain parts of their bodies
- feel uncomfortable in hot weather
- struggle to keep up with others

Being overweight can lead to **high blood pressure**, heart disease, and a condition called Type 2 **diabetes**.

What is BMI?

A common way to measure whether adults are overweight is to check their body mass index (BMI). This is worked out by doing a sum using someone's height and weight. When a child's BMI is **calculated**, the sum needs to take into account age and gender.

The higher the BMI, the higher the risk of developing health problems connected to being overweight. However, BMI is just a number, and people are not numbers. Doctors also consider your background when they decide if you have a healthy BMI. BMI doesn't adjust for fat or muscle; for this reason, BMI is not a good measure for athletes.

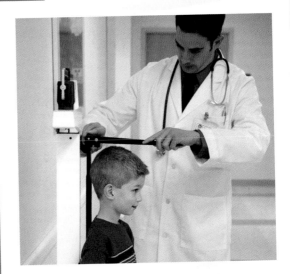

Other measurements

Another common measure used for adults is the size of their waist. A large waist size can be a sign of unhealthy fat stored around the stomach. This is important because "tummy fat" is connected to health problems such as diabetes.

Working out whether someone is overweight is much more complicated than just jumping on the scales to see how much they weigh.

Good balance

People are overweight for lots of reasons. The most obvious one is simple math. You gain weight when your body takes in more energy than it burns up. Keeping a diary of eating and exercise—an E-diary—can help you to see if you have the right balance of food and activity.

Archie isn't eating more than his friends, but he's gaining weight. Check out his E-diary.

Archie's Friday E-diary

8:00 am	Slept in. Skipped breakfast.
8:30 am	Mom drove me to bus stop.
10:05 am	Had a piece of pie during morning break.
10:20 am	Played trading-card game with Max and Henry.
12:15 pm	Hot dog, juice box, and fruit candy for lunch.
12:35 pm	Sat with Max and played video game.
3:45 pm	Walked from bus stop. Had chocolate milk and a granola bar for afternoon snack.
4:00 pm	Did homework.
5:00 pm	Played computer game.
6:30 pm	For dinner, had roast beef and potatoes with gravy, then apple pie and ice cream.
7:00 pm	Watched TV.
8:00 pm	Had milk and chocolate cookie for a snack. Watched some more TV.
8:30 pm	Bed.

Too much food plus not enough exercise adds up to extra weight.

Joe eats plenty of food, but he maintains a healthy weight. Can you explain why?

Joe's Friday E-diary

7:30 am	Breakfast of cereal with milk and banana, and orange juice.
8:30 am	Walked to school with Nick.
10:05 am	In the morning, had yogurt, a muffin, and an apple.
10:20 am	Played basketball with Nick and Frances. Drank water.
12:15 pm	For lunch, had a ham sandwich, orange, hard-boiled egg, and water.
12:35 pm	Kicked the ball around with the guys.
3:45 pm	Walked home with Nick. Snacked on carrot and celery sticks with some dip and a glass of milk.
4:00 pm	Did homework.
5:00 pm	Played around on my skateboard and shot some baskets.
6:30 pm	For dinner had pasta with meat sauce and vegetables. Dessert was low-fat ice cream with strawberries.
7:30 pm	Watched TV.
8:00 pm	Munched on some fresh pineapple.
8:30 pm	Bed.

Aim to be active for an hour or more every day. Sports and gym class are important, but what else do you do? If you're like Archie, you could start by walking more. Take a jump rope to school and get your friends involved. Just get moving!

It runs in the family

Many body features are passed on to us by our **ancestors**. What shape we are is partly decided before we are born. Being overweight can run in families. Our family's habits are passed on to us, too—even the bad ones! Although it is not always easy, habits can be changed.

September 3

Dear Diary,

"Overweight" is such a gross word. Dad says I'm cuddly, Mom says I'm nicely rounded, and Hayley, the popular kid at school, says I make her look good in the class photo.

I don't like having my photo taken when I'm in a bathing suit, but I did come in third in the swimming relay. Got the "best effort" ribbon.

September 5

Then came the BIG problem. Yep, the school medical exam. It was SO gross.

Doctors measure AND weigh you. I was off the end of the scale for my age—SO embarrassing! The nurse was really nice about it.

Classmates joke that I should enter that TV show where people **diet** to lose the most weight and win MILLIONS! In their dreams.

September 7

Dear Diary,

Today was the WORST! Dad was rushed to the hospital after a heart attack. Can't write. Too upset.

September 12

Dear Diary,

Phew! Dad is going to be OK. The doctors had long talks with us all and Mom says things are going to change around here. She has a pile of low-fat, low-sugar recipes and has bought us all way-cool sneakers so we can go walking together. Even the dog is excited!

November 7

Dear Diary,

Mom wasn't kidding about the changes around here. I'm allowed to ride to school. I don't have to finish everything on my plate anymore. We even have smaller plates! I've tried about a zillion different fruits and veggies. Mango is yum!

Me riding my bike to school

December 12

Dear Diary,

This is going to be the BEST vacation ever! We've all lost heaps of weight. Dad's blood pressure is where it should be, plus we have the fittest dog on the block! Mom took me shopping yesterday for new clothes. I loved trying on all the fun stuff that never fit me before. And guess what?? I'm going to be captain of the swim team next year. Eating healthy food and being active is awesome. I've never been happier. Hayley had better watch out!

Which path will YOU take?

START

Life is a journey. Follow the right signs and it's easy to choose the best path to health success.

GOOD EATING HABITS

Eat a good breakfast so you will:

- wake up the inside of your body
- work better during the day
- not get so hungry later
- be in a better mood

MyPyramid
STEPS TO A HEALTHIER YOU
MyPyramid.gov

GRAINS   VEGETABLES   FRUITS   MILK   MEAT & BEANS

Try peanut butter on toast or oatmeal with banana for breakfast.

Beat the snack attacks by planning ahead. Fruit is the easiest, fastest food to snack on. But why not prepare some fabulous munchies for when you need to nibble? Try:

- dried fruit plus pumpkin seeds (remember that dried fruit has more energy than fresh fruit)
- natural popcorn

- crackers with peanut butter or cream cheese
- toasted or baked pita bread with hummus
- sticks of carrot, celery, green beans, peppers, and zucchini

FINISH

Eat sensibly and stay active. That way, you will make the most of whatever shape and size you are!

YOU CAN DO IT!

Set realistic goals so you can:

- see your progress
- build your self-confidence
- enjoy your success

NO EXCUSES

Ban these excuses from your life:

- It's boring.
- I'm too tired.
- I'm no good at that.
- I don't feel like it.
- I need to watch my favorite TV show.

ACTION

Keep moving because exercise:

- improves the working of your heart and lungs
- burns extra energy
- makes you feel good about yourself
- helps you challenge yourself

ACTION — EXCUSES

Which path will you choose?

Diet is for life

Many people think the word "diet" means not eating food or restricting the amount of food you eat. Actually your diet is not what you DON'T eat; it's everything you DO eat. Having a good diet means having a balanced eating plan. Good diet is a lifelong habit, not something you do for a short while.

The big losers

Turn on the television almost any day and you will see advertisements for weight-loss programs and people talking about how they want to be slimmer. There is even a reality show about people who compete to lose the most weight in a short time. They stop eating certain types of food, severely reduce the amount they eat, and overexercise to win the competition. Contestants risk their good health while millions of people sit in their living rooms and watch (maybe even while snacking!).

Dieting can cause big problems. If your body thinks it's starving, it will store more energy as fat and slow down the rate at which it works. You can end up even more overweight than you were before you started. You can also become ill if you don't get all the foods you need.

Crash diets are well named. Go on one and your health will crash!

Diet myth-busting

People say and believe all sorts of strange things about dieting and food. Some people are looking for an easy, quick solution. However, there are no magic foods that make weight drop off or cure disease! Here are some common food **myths**.

Water versus soft drinks

If you drink while you eat, you gain more weight.

Busted: Not if you drink water.

Fruit fiction

Bananas are fattening.

Busted: A banana contains around half a gram of fat. Athletes love them.

Vegetable Tale

Vegetarians are healthier.

Busted: Vegetarians can make bad food choices, too!

Sunny snacks

Citrus fruits have the most vitamin C.

Busted: A raw red pepper has twice as much vitamin C as an orange.

Too much of anything —even low-fat foods—can make you gain weight!

How much is enough?

We all know that we should be eating healthy foods, but sometimes we find it hard to know what that means. We might know what is best to eat but have trouble changing our bad eating habits. We might choose the best foods, but eat too much or too little of them. The best way to stay on track is to plan ahead. Families should make a healthy-eating plan each week and use it to make the shopping list.

Eating plans

Grab some cookbooks and food magazines and find healthy recipes that your family will enjoy. Most recipes tell you how many servings they make. Use that as a guide to make sure you eat the right amount of food.

Now plan breakfast, lunch, and dinner for the week. List the **ingredients** and shop for what you need. When you do this, you'll be amazed by how many different and interesting foods are healthy. Healthy eating is not boring eating.

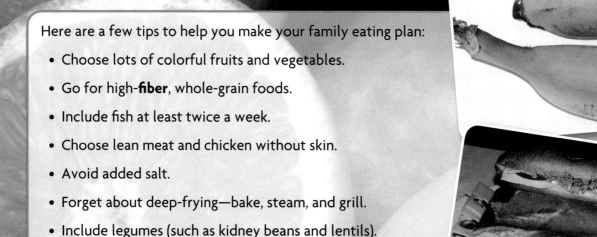

Here are a few tips to help you make your family eating plan:

- Choose lots of colorful fruits and vegetables.
- Go for high-**fiber**, whole-grain foods.
- Include fish at least twice a week.
- Choose lean meat and chicken without skin.
- Avoid added salt.
- Forget about deep-frying—bake, steam, and grill.
- Include legumes (such as kidney beans and lentils).
- Select low-fat dairy products.
- Use olive oil instead of butter.

The Hunger Meter

A good way to make sure you eat the right amount is to use the Hunger Meter. Imagine that your stomach is a tank with ten levels. At level 1, it is almost empty and you feel extremely hungry. At level 10, it is absolutely stuffed. You could not fit in another tiny drop!

When your stomach is between levels 4 and 7, it is filled to a healthy level. So you should start to refuel when you get down around level 3 and stop when you reach level 7. Use the Hunger Meter for a while, and you will soon find it uncomfortable to be out of the healthy range.

The Hunger Meter

Stuffed

Full

Healthy

Low

Running-
on-empty

> If hunger is not the problem, then food is not the solution.

Eating disorders

What are they?

Eating disorders are illnesses related to eating and food. People with eating disorders do not have healthy eating patterns or attitudes toward food. They find it hard to think about anything other than their weight and body shape. They often use extreme methods to gain or lose weight.

Can eating disorders be fixed?

Yes, they can, but only with help from doctors and support from family and friends.

Bulimia nervosa

People suffering from bulimia nervosa struggle to control how much they eat. They regularly eat a large amount of food at one time, often in secret ("binge eating"). Then they feel bad about it. They try to get rid of the food by vomiting, overexercising, starving themselves, or even taking pills.

Anorexia nervosa

People experiencing anorexia nervosa can't think about anything else but being thin. The usual signs are being underweight for their age and height, and thinking they are fat even when they are very thin.

What causes eating disorders?

There is no simple answer to this question. Some possibilities are:

- dieting that gets out of control
- **emotional** problems
- trying to look like someone you admire
- **stress**

What causes stress?

When you are anxious, nervous, and under pressure, you feel stress. Common causes of stress might be:

- tests and exams
- your parents splitting up
- moving
- changing schools
- being bullied
- having trouble with friendships

URGENT

Dear Mom,

I had to go to bed, but I needed to talk to you about a big problem. I am worried about my school friend Mira, who is getting a lot thinner. I thought she might have anorexia nervosa. I am determined to get Mira to talk about anything that might be troubling her.

Mira trusted me enough to tell me that she thought everyone would like her more if she was thinner. I said, "You don't need to be thinner. Your friends like you just as you are."

I am really worried about Mira losing too much weight, so should I speak to our teacher about it? Or should I speak to Mira's parents?

Can I talk to you about this before I leave for school tomorrow?

What can you do to help if your friend has an eating disorder? You can:

- let them know how you feel about them
- listen
- share ideas
- encourage them to talk to a doctor or their family
- always be there

A world of difference

What difference do they make?

Does your family come from another country? That can make a BIG difference in what you eat every day.

Italy
pasta with a rich tomato sauce

France
Traditional French food is high in **calories** but people tend to eat small servings.

Lebanon
tabouleh

India
spicy curry with dahl

Where your family comes from can make a difference to the shape and weight of your body. If you are a Pacific Islander or an African American, for example, your healthy size is likely to be larger than if you are an **Indigenous** Australian. We are all different. Life would be pretty dull otherwise!

Cultures around the world have everyday foods based on the meats, grains, and crops that grow where they live. Rice, lentils, pasta, noodles, all types of bread, meat, and fish are enjoyed with hundreds of fruits and vegetables, spices, and sauces. There's a whole world of flavors out there and many ways to enjoy a **balanced diet**. Be adventurous! It's fun.

Russia
borscht — thick beet soup with sour cream

Vietnam
stir-fry with noodles and fish sauce

United States
The first course in a traditional American meal is a salad.

The ideal weight and healthy BMI is lower for Asian people than for European people.

Why not try some healthy eating from other lands?

Feelings and food

In memories, food is often linked to events and people. Your grandmother might bake the best cookies in the world. The smell of a barbecue might remind you of your last vacation. The way you feel—your emotions—can be connected with food in positive and negative ways.

You're invited *to think about how important food is to celebration times. When we celebrate special events in our lives, we have special foods. These are often high-sugar and high-fat foods. They're treats, or "sometimes" foods. "Sometimes" does not mean "every day."*

Where *we get together for a special meal with people we care about may be a home, restaurant, or park. We sit around the table to talk and laugh together. The food is not really the important thing—the people are. We take our time and enjoy each other's company.*

When *possible, take the time to think about the real reason for the celebration. Remember the occasion for the warm way you feel, knowing you are loved, not for that piece of chocolate cake!*

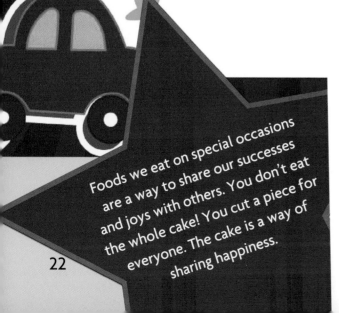

Foods we eat on special occasions are a way to share our successes and joys with others. You don't eat the whole cake! You cut a piece for everyone. The cake is a way of sharing happiness.

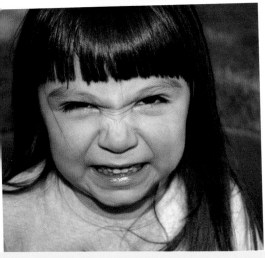

"Eww, yuck!" is not a feeling. It's a reaction. Sometimes you need to try new things several times before you like them.

Some people eat because they're bored. Wouldn't it be a better idea to cook for the family? That way you are busy doing something worthwhile and fun.

Don't stop eating because you're confused or worried. Talk to someone you trust about the problem.

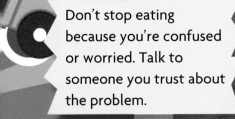

OK, so being greedy isn't a feeling either. It's a habit. However, the resulting stomachache might be a feeling! If you want something sweet or high in calories once in a while, go ahead! Just remember to have a small portion.

Some foods are called "comfort foods" because they make us feel warm and comfortable. When we were babies, we felt safe and loved when Mom or Dad cuddled us as we were fed. Food doesn't love us; people do. Have a hug instead of those chips!

Do you feel up or down?

Fresh, natural food and water helps give us:

- higher energy
- a healthy body weight
- improved sleep
- better concentration

With so many processed and fast foods available, we have to know how to make good health choices.

Try this healthy snakes-and-ladders game.

17

18

19
You eat six chocolate cookies after school.

20

16
You buy a big bag of chips and eat the whole bag while watching TV.

15

14

1 Start

2

3
It's a rainy day, but you exercise inside by dancing.

4

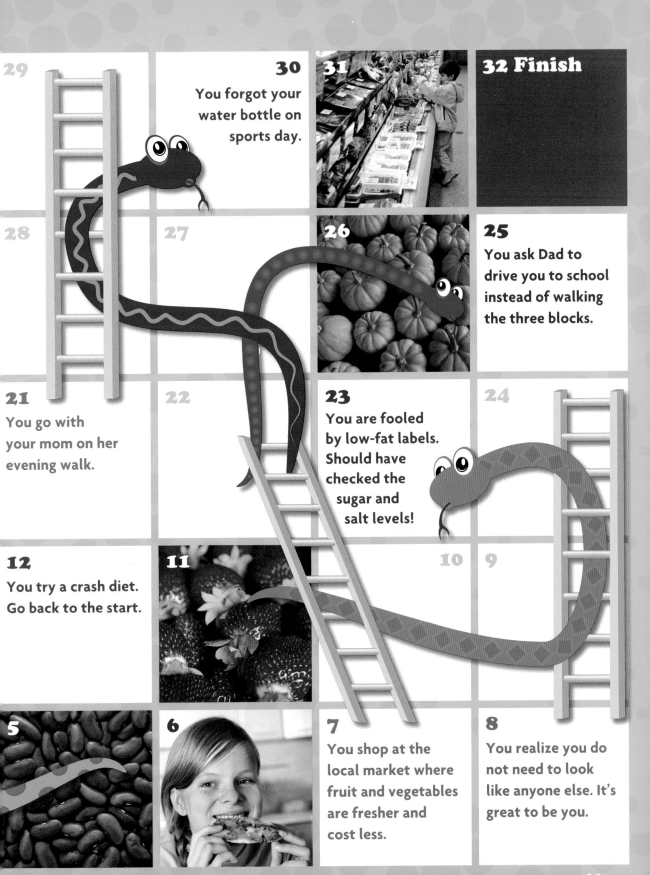

29

30 You forgot your water bottle on sports day.

31

32 Finish

28

27

26

25 You ask Dad to drive you to school instead of walking the three blocks.

21 You go with your mom on her evening walk.

22

23 You are fooled by low-fat labels. Should have checked the sugar and salt levels!

24

12 You try a crash diet. Go back to the start.

11

10

9

5

6

7 You shop at the local market where fruit and vegetables are fresher and cost less.

8 You realize you do not need to look like anyone else. It's great to be you.

Fast food is not all junk

Once upon a time, when your grandparents were children, there were no fast-food restaurants.

Hard to imagine, isn't it? Take away the take-out dinners, and lots of working parents would be extra tired. Lots of kids would be extra disappointed, too!

What is junk food?

Junk is another word for garbage: something you throw away because it has no use. That's not how we should think about food. Food is essential fuel. Junk food contains very little **nutritional** value. It doesn't have much that is actually good for you, such as vitamins, **protein**, or fiber. What it usually does contain is lots of salt, fat, sugar, and even chemicals. Lollipops, potato chips, and soft drinks all qualify as junk food.

What about fast food?

Fast food is just what it sounds like—food that is ready in a hurry. Fast food has been prepared for you to save you the time it takes to cook. That doesn't mean it has to be junk. Many fast food companies produce low-fat, low-sugar foods, and many restaurants offer take-out service for tasty, healthy meals.

So what's the problem?

The problem is the choices you make, not the food itself. There's no problem if you most often choose foods with good nutritional value and eat junk only rarely.

Fast choices

Problem:

My family has fried fish and french fries for dinner almost every Friday night. I know all that deep-fried food is not a great idea, but I'm not allowed in the kitchen to cook for myself. What should I do?

Solution:

Did you know that the original reason fish was covered in batter and thrown into the deep-fryer with the potato was to cook the fish without drying it out? Inside that fatty batter is lovely, moist, steamed fish. So you could try eating a few fries, taking the fish out of the batter, and asking if you can add some salad. Perhaps you could ask to have your fish grilled. Perhaps the take-out restaurant makes something else that you could order instead.

Problem:

I go to sports training straight after school. I barely have time to walk home and get changed before I have to head out the door again. I have to walk past the fast-food restaurants to reach home. What would be a good fast food for me to grab?

Solution:

You don't want to fill your stomach up before serious exercising, but you do need to put some fuel in your tank to keep you going. **Carbohydrates** and proteins are essential. Sushi or nori rolls would be a wise choice. They are packed with nutrition and have very little fat content to bog you down.

Thin-crust vegetable pizza, low-fat frozen yogurt, ready-made salads with grilled chicken, steamed rice with braised meat and vegetables, bread with dips, multigrain sandwiches, fruit muffins, chicken and avocado wraps, falafel . . . **there are endless choices of fast food that are not junk.**

How to Manage Weight

Food

- Get involved in planning the weekly menus for your family.
- Learn how to cook so you really know what ingredients are in foods.
- Eat slowly.
- Don't have big portions.
- Eat different types of food.
- Choose healthy snacks.

Exercise

- Find fun ways to be active: juggle, skip, dance, bounce.
- Suggest leaving the car at home and walk or bike.
- Take up a new sport, such as jogging, karate, diving.

Get a good night's sleep

- Don't stay up late playing video games or watching TV.
- Get up early and keep busy all day so that you are ready to sleep at night.

Get involved

- Join in things at school and after school so that you can spend more time with other kids having fun—swimming, dancing, skateboarding, riding, hiking . . .

Make the most of yourself

- You only get one body, so look after it and feel good about it.

Be happy

- Staying positive helps you reach your goals.
- Remember, everyone has bad days.
- Don't sit and be sad. Get active and you really will feel better afterwards.

Award for Friendship

If your friend has a problem being overweight, then you can be a good friend by:

- eating healthy food yourself
- encouraging your friend to join in sports
- helping them practice sports skills
- not criticizing
- making sure you remind your friend about all their good points
- talking about feelings
- inviting your friend to do fun things with you
- telling the teacher if your friend is being teased or called unkind names (no one should have to put up with bullies)
- not discussing your friend's problems with outsiders
- being honest and positive

Remember the story about the race between the tortoise and the hare? The hare thought he was so fast and clever that he stopped to rest. The slow and steady tortoise just kept on going and passed him by. Staying on track and being true to yourself are winning strategies.

15-point plan to stay healthy

1 Eat five servings of vegetables and two of fruit every day.

2 Be active for one hour a day.

3 Walk whenever possible.

4 Plan ahead.

5 Find friends to exercise with.

6 Choose low-fat foods.

7 Drink water instead of sug soft drinks.

8 Set goals you can achieve.

9 Watch TV or play computer games for no more than one hour a day.

10 Eat sensibly sized meals.

11 Never miss breakfast.

Munch on fruit and vegetables, not chocolate and chips.

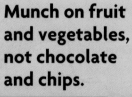

30

12

13 Learn to say "No thanks."

14 Share your feelings with others.

15 Remember to have fun!

Glossary

ancestors	the members of your family who lived a long time before you
balanced diet	meals that give you the best combination of healthy foods
calculate	work something out, such as a sum
calorie	unit to measure energy
carbohydrates	starch and sugar foods; pasta and bread contain carbohydrates
citrus	fruits related to orange, lemon, lime, and grapefruit
diabetes	an illness that causes high levels of sugar in a person's blood
diet	the foods you eat
dieting	limiting the sort and amount of food you eat
emotional	having to do with feelings
energy	fuel for activity
fiber	rough part of foods that is not taken in by the body but helps other foods to be better taken in
good health	without disease and with a body and mind that are in good condition
high blood pressure	an illness in which the blood puts too much pressure on the walls of blood vessels
indigenous	native
ingredients	elements that go into making something
internal organs	parts of the body that have a particular purpose, such as lungs, heart, kidneys, and liver
muscles	body parts that help you move and give you strength
myths	stories from long ago
nutritional	providing the kinds of food to keep you healthy
overweight	heavier than the healthy average
protein	an important part of food found in eggs, meat, fish, or poultry
stress	pressure or worry you feel
vegetarians	people who do not eat meat, fish, or poultry
vitamin	something found in many foods and needed for good health

For Further Information

Books

Claybourne, Anna. *Healthy Eating: Diet and Nutrition*. Portsmouth, NH: Heinemann, 2008.

Kern, Merilee. *Making Healthy Choices: A Story to Inspire Fit, Weight-Wise Kids*. Tucson, AZ: Wheatmark Publishers, 2006.

Web Sites

MyPyramid.gov: For Kids

www.mypyramid.gov/kids/

What's the Right Weight for Me?

kidshealth.org/kid/feeling/thought/fat_thin.html

Publisher's note to educators and parents: Our editors have carefully reviewed these Web sites to ensure that they are suitable for students. Many Web sites change frequently, however, and we cannot guarantee that a site's future contents will continue to meet our high standards of quality and educational value. Be advised that students should be closely supervised whenever they access the Internet.

Index